I

While ... were ... chasing the next
new-new internet tricks, a group of UK strategists and designers – led by Sarah Richards – had
quietly redefined the standards for how a government could serve its constituents online. And they
didn't do it with fancy technology, 'innovative'
design, or a horde of expensive consultants: they
did it with words.

Our industry pays a lot of lip-service to 'user-centered content.' Put the user first, we say. Anticipate
their needs. Prioritize their preferences. Deliver
delightful experiences! The problem is that all too
often, we don't actually spend the time or money
to find out what our users really, truly care about
in the first place. As deadlines loom, we begin to
allow our assumptions drive the bus. 'We already
know our users, because we've been serving them
for such a long time.' Or, 'Our research didn't really
give us quite the right information, but we'll just
use what we have for now.'

Good web teams aren't lazy about research. They
aren't satisfied with half-baked personas. They
don't just kick content out the door and move on
to the next thing. They are relentless about asking
better questions, analyzing data, and iterative
improvement. They're in it for the long haul, and
they're in it for the user. That's essentially why
GOV.UK succeeds. It's why content strategists

around the world point to the site again and again as an example of what can be done if you are brave enough to let user-centered content lead the way.

And it does take courage. When you are reinventing an online service from the ground up, there's nowhere to hide. Either you nail it or you don't. Sarah's team nailed it, and they did it with the most straightforward, honest approach to design I've ever seen. They defined measurable goals, identified key obstacles, navigated them with data-based decisions, and delivered an unparalleled user experience ... designed solely with content. What's more, they did it out in the open, bringing the rest of us along for the ride. That work continues today, in no part thanks to Sarah's visionary articulation of the value of content design.

Sarah is a consummate problem-solver. Her work in content design has given us a flexible set of tools to identify, articulate, and meet our users' most important needs. Above all else, she is pragmatic in her work – she has no time for silver bullets or 'the next big thing.' She's straightforward in her approach and unrelenting in her pursuit of simplicity, both in her own instruction and in what she delivers to the user.

All that said: she knows her readers. She knows we are word fanatics. That we strive 24/7 to empathize with our audiences. That, more than anything, we want to do meaningful work that contributes to the success of both our users and our organizations. We are her audience. And she's done the hard work to help us succeed. This book is the result of that hard work. Read it, re-read it, and keep it close at hand. It will help you build a better web.

Kristina Halvorson
May 2017

Founder, Brain Traffic and Confab Events
Author, Content Strategy for the Web

This book explains content design

It will tell you what content design means, how it's different from copywriting, and how to make it work successfully in your organisation.

It takes you through the content design process, one step at a time, with frequent reference to fictional examples and to real-world situations I've encountered during my career.

This book is not about content strategy, the process that gives you an idea of what you are publishing where and why.

Ideally, you should understand your content strategy before you start working on content design.

Content strategy is a subject of its own, and someone else has already written the book on it: I recommend <u>Content Strategy for the Web</u> by Kristina Halvorson and Melissa Rach.

This book is not about design as in graphics, icons, look and feel, colours, interaction and so on. It's about the content that sits within the design.

Contents

Preparation

Designing

Content design

Introduction

Defining content design

Content design means not limiting yourself to just words. Content on the web is often words, but not always. The point of content design is that you start with research to help you identify what your users actually need (which isn't the same as what they say they want).

Then instead of saying 'How shall I write this?', you say, 'What content will best meet this need?'

The answer might be words, but it might also be other things: pictures, diagrams, charts, links, calendars, a series of questions and answers, videos, addresses, maps, calculators, spreadsheets, printable documents, and many more besides.

When your job is to decide which one of those, or which combination of several of them, meets the user's need – that's content design.

A quick history of publishing

Humans have been communicating for a long

time – cave paintings can be dated back 40,000 years. The first writing systems are thought to have emerged in ancient Sumer (modern-day Iraq) around 3200 BC. Since then, humans have evolved, adapted, lost and revamped their communication techniques. But one thing has stayed the same: we want other people to consume our thoughts, feelings, goods and services, and we'll adapt to make that happen.

Fast-forward to today: the internet is a (relatively) new thing, and for the most part we're still adapting to make best use of it. In the early days, many people assumed that publishing online just meant taking everything that already existed offline, on paper, and just shoving it on a website. (Some are still doing this.)

But that approach doesn't work well.

Since developing paper, the printing press and books, the process of publishing was:
- writer writes
- editor edits
- printer prints

Easy. All nicely defined in a lovely linear process.

In the early days of the web, some online publishing worked like this:
- writer writes
- writer publishes (with or without editing or sign-off)

That was brilliant. We could all publish our thoughts

faster. We didn't have lengthy subbing processes or months to wait for something to be designed and printed. We were reading faster, publishing faster, learning faster, becoming a community faster.

As the search engines themselves got better, we had to work harder to make our websites stand out. The concept of search engine optimisation (SEO) was born, and many web content producers took it to heart.

Online publishing in lots of places now looks like this:
- writer writes
- SEO team adds SEO keywords
- editor edits
- legal expert signs off
- publishing team publishes

Which is much better. And to be fair, a lot of organisations do well with this process. But it has some flaws.

Want vs need

The 'write, SEO, sub, publish' type of publishing doesn't necessarily take into account what users actually need. Sometimes, users don't **need** to read anything. What a user wants and what they need might be two different things.

For example, a person may want a quick, easy solution to a complicated debt problem.

What they **need**, however, is a series of easy-to-follow steps to get them out of debt – which may not be quick or easy at all. It's not what the person wants, but it is what they need.

A content designer will think about the best possible way to deliver information to the indebted person. Perhaps that might mean using video, or an online debt repayments calculator. Those are pieces of content that might meet the need, but in many organisations, creating them will be the responsibility of a completely different team.

So a content design approach will take that into account, and the work might involve building relationships with teams you've not worked with before.

Business needs vs user needs

A business usually needs money to run. Even if the goal is simply to help people, at some point almost all businesses need money to function. Sometimes what a user wants gets forgotten in a lot of pages saying what the business or organisation wants to say.

I'll show you how to keep your business and user needs in mind and how to tackle both together.

What content designers are like

There's a lot of technical skill in content design.

You have to know how to interpret analytical data, and how to put that data to good work. It can tell you things that help you plan your content. You have to be aware of all forms of communication that could be useful, and you have to know a lot about your audience to know what is right for them. We'll go through it all in this book.

I think good content designers:
- should be humble; they serve the audience
- are totally focused on user-centred content
- appreciate that no one can know everything
- are open to learning
- aren't wedded to grammar rules they were taught in primary school. Language moves on and a good content designer moves on with it

Humans learn, evolve and adapt and you need to adapt with them. Assume nothing, question everything and test until you are sure.

Then go and do it again.

Because that's how content design works.

Finding your way through this book

This book is divided into 2 halves.

The first 5 chapters are about preparatory work - doing research and going through the essential discovery phase.

Chapters 6 to 10 are more practical, guiding you through the tasks you'll need to complete one at a time.

Why content design matters

A few years ago, I worked on a website that had a page designed to help people find their local GP.

The problem was that most people don't say 'GP', they say 'doctor'. When they search on the web, they use 'doctor' there too.

Users weren't finding the right page on the website because it didn't have the word 'doctor' on it.

I changed the term and the page went from being in the bottom 50 for the whole site, to one of the top pages.

That's iterative content design in action.

As so many organisations are still focused on what messages they want to push, rather than what their users need...

why do you
need to put so
much effort into
your content?

Organisations like Apple, Amazon and Google take research and user behaviour seriously.

They are also global, very successful brands people talk about.

They are successful because they make people happy, which includes creating websites that are easy to use and meet people's needs.

There are billions &
billions &
billions &
billions &
billions &
billions &
billions &
billions &
billions &
billions &
billions &
billions &
billions &
billions of
pages on the internet.

Unless you are
a unique entity
that people have
no choice but to
deal with

the UK government, for instance

you have
competitors.

To do better than your
competitors, you need
smarter content.

Not more content,

smarter content

Writing digital content is a skill. People won't find your website because your design is funky.

They'll use words they are thinking about and pick you from a swarm of other results offered up by search engines.

You need to stand out on the results page.

That's why content design is important: it helps you stand out in a world where everyone wants to stand out.

Standing out comes down to three things:
- push vs pull content
- trust
- ease of use

Let's look at each one of those in turn.

Push vs pull content

There are two types of writing for communications: push and pull.

Push content

If you see a poster while waiting for a bus, you are choosing to look at it, but it is there. It's in front of you. The effort is minimal. Your eyes just happen to hit it. Similarly, if you publish a press release and send it to every journalist you know, that's push content. Content is being shoved out there for someone to pick up.

Pull content

When you go to a website, you are pulling the content. To get to a page at all, you have to decide what you want to read about, get some words in mind, type them into a search engine, choose from the results, and then get to a page to consume the content. You might see a link on another page or Twitter and decide you want to follow that link to read the content. All of that takes effort. All of that means you actually have to do something. That's pull content. You pull the content towards you.

The most important skill for writing on the web is

turning push content (what you want to say) into pull content (what your audience wants to read).

Any push content can be turned to pull. All you need to do is find what your audience actually wants. The more pull your content has, the more successful you will be. For example:

Push:

Look at this cool new phone! Buy it!

Pull:

This cool new phone makes your life easier and puts the entire world in your pocket. And it's only £500.

Books would be boring if there were no thought-provoking prose. And adverts wouldn't persuade us to buy anything if they just said: 'Trainers. Keep your feet dry. Available in two colours.'

But for either type of communication to be successful, it has to be what the intended audience wants or needs at the time they see it.

Trust

If your audience doesn't trust you, they won't interact with you – it's as simple as that. While you gain trust from your reputation, track record and marketing on the web, trust can come from:

- design (does it look like the real deal or is it a scam site?)
- brand awareness (does it match your brand? If the Ministry of Justice looked and felt like Ministry of Sound, people wouldn't trust it, would they?)
- content quality (people don't trust sites with poor spelling)

If your site doesn't offer these things, people will find the information or service somewhere else. If that's not possible, they will try to find a workaround, or just complain about it. Either way, you have lost them.

Ease of use

Making your site easy to understand and interact with is the fastest way to a happy audience.

Of course, all those things are relative. An academic might want 100,000 words on a new theory in their field of expertise and they will find technical language easy to digest.

A debt-troubled parent worrying about putting food on the table won't want 100,000 words on the history of the credit crunch in the UK. They need 300 words telling them that help is available and where to find it.

Knowing your audience will tell you what they need.

Content design in action

If you want to book a UK driving test online, the cheapest way is through the official government website. A few years ago, the booking service was awful. People used to go to other providers, who put better design and interaction on top of the booking service, but also charged extra fees.

A lot of users didn't realise that the official government site was a cheaper alternative. They ended up needlessly paying more. Others did know about the official site, but still used the third-party alternatives – for them, it was worth paying extra just to avoid using the the clunky government service.

The official site is now much improved, but the lesson learned is a powerful one: sometimes, people will knowingly pay more if the interaction is easier.

If you publish push content and care more about your organisation's internal workings than what your audience needs, you are going to be left behind because:

- your audience won't find you in the first place (you'll be too far down the search results)
- if it's easier to get the information or service from somewhere else, people will
- you will sustain reputational damage. The web is a wonderful place for ranting and criticism; it doesn't take much to hurt an organisation

The science
of reading

A good content designer understands a bit about the involuntary mechanics that govern how humans take in information.

The better you understand how that happens,
the more likely you will be able to write content
that's easy to read.

It's a useful problem-solving tool as well; if research shows that a piece of content isn't working, it might be because of how humans work.

Knowing how to fix things like that will save you a lot of time in the long run.

What happens when eyes look at words

There are entire books you can read about the science of reading. But let's just summarise the stuff that matters to you as a content designer.

Think about what reading involves. Is it that you are looking at letters, forming words in your mind and taking meaning before moving on to the next word? Well, sort of.

A definition of reading in Keith Rayner and Alexander Pollatsek's Psychology of Reading states: 'Reading is the ability to extract visual information from the page and comprehend the meaning of the text.'

Most of the western, literate world reads in exactly the same way. The human brain just works like that. It's only if you have cognitive or physical impairments that this process changes.

A reader's eyes don't simply read one word and then move on to the next. Rather, they jump about all over the place. When the eye lands on a place or word, that's called a fixation. Fixations happen in 3 zones:

- one where you read the first few characters of a word (it can take 100 milliseconds (ms) for the

Lots of writers have no idea how we consume information - we watch research and change things accordingly. But did you know most of how we 'read' is pathological? You don't have much control over it. If a piece of content isn't working in research, you might be able to find out why based on how humans work, not just what that person is thinking at that time, and so you'll save time in the long run.

reader's brain to identify a word)
- the second zone gives you more information about the word and any small function words to the right
- the third zone (known as your parafoveal view) tells you where might be best for the next fixation point

The more familiar your words are to the reader, the faster the reader can understand what they mean.

When the eye jumps, that's known as a saccade (pronounced 'sa-kaid').

People only take in information on the fixation, not the saccade. You can see for yourself: go to a mirror and try to watch your eyes move. They will move, but you won't see the movement. You'll only be able to take in visual

So your eyes jump about all over the place and your brain makes up content during the jumps. It fills in the gaps. From the age of 9, your eyes can miss 30% of text on a page and your brain will still accurately predict the content. That's not device-specific. That's just what happens. That's how humans work.

In his study 'How Little Do Users Read?', Jakob Nielsen found that online, people only read 20–28% of the page. The cognitive load (in other words, the mental effort required to take in the information) increases 11% for every 100 words added to the page. So how do people actually get information from the page?

You've probably seen the Jakob Nielsen eye-tracking heat maps that show the F-shaped pattern for websites on the desktop. You'll notice that, generally, on whatever site you have, whatever you are offering, the first couple of sentences are at least skimmed.

Memory

Words are stored like long-term memories, just like sounds and smells. You have probably had the experience when a smell has revived a memory you've not thought about in years, or a sound sparks a long-

...r public

...work for certain public duties as ...normal holiday entitlement. Employers can choose to pay th... time, but they don't have to.

...take time off for jury s...

...alifies for time off

An ...loyee can get a 'reasonable' amount of time off if the...

- a magistrate (also known as a justice of the peace)
- ...cal councillor
- ...ool governor
- ...mber of any statutory tribunal (for example an employ...
- a member of the managing or governing body of an educat... establishment
- a member of a health authority
- a member of a school council or board in Scotland
- a member of the General Teaching Councils for England ar...
- a member of the Environment Agency or the Scottish Envi... Protection agency
- a member of the prison independent monitoring boards (E...

repressed birthday party image or similar – it's all there, it's all in your long-term memory.

The more our brains practise something, the deeper the impression it leaves and the stronger the memory.

The more you read – the deeper the impression words have on your mind – the easier it is to recall them. That means readers can recognise words on the third eye fixation zone, which means they read faster.

You can use this to your advantage when designing content: there's a strong argument for using words your readers can easily recognise, understand and skip by using their natural saccade rhythm.

Which words to use

Most people have a common vocabulary of around 15,000 terms. These are words a reader's eyes are more likely to easily skip because they are so recognisable. If you have children and they come home from school with 'high-frequency word lists', that's the start of that vocabulary.

By using these words, you allow your users to take in more information at a more rapid pace. This is often called 'using plain English'. Or by some people, 'dumbing down'.

It's not
dumbing down

it's opening up

www.breakingeverything.gov.uk · Government Digital Service

Low-frequency words take about 100ms longer to read than high-frequency words. In one study, participants were shown the words 'coat' and 'cove'. Coat is in everyday language. Cove isn't.

Most high-frequency words in English are function words, like prepositions, conjunctions, pronouns (and, the, on, but, by, me, she, it). Low-frequency words are usually nouns, verbs and adjectives (kettle, making, lovely). You need both to form sentences, but if you keep language to the common terms where possible, you are allowing your users to read more quickly.

Typography

There have been many studies that show the effects of typography on reading speed and comprehension.

In 1969, Smith, Lott and Cronnell completed a study on AlTeRnAtInG TeXt LiKe ThIs, claiming that word identification was not impaired by printing words in a mixture of upper and lower cases. But in 1974, Coltheart and Freeman re-examined that study's methodology and declared it was on average 12ms slower to make a word decision.

However, later studies (Paveea and Rosa, 2002) showed greater effects. The main problem with this type of study is that it is difficult to know if the delay is due to word identification or just because it looks odd and unfamiliar. A new study showing this and perhaps looking into the effects of modern-day design on our perception of what is familiar would be beneficial.

Text presented in sentence case is the most familiar style for most people and, therefore, usually the fastest to read.

Between 10 and 15% of saccades are regressive saccades, also known as return path reading. Eyes bounce backwards over the text because the reader didn't take it in the first time. This happens in fractions of seconds. Most readers probably aren't even aware they're doing it. Most probably do 4 to 5 saccades per second, and a regression once every 2 seconds.

This leads to a typographical consideration. If lines of text are too short, you'll increase regressive saccades. If they are too long, the return path is too long and people can get confused about where their eye needs to go back to.

The size of the text doesn't matter: studies show saccades stay about the same.

So what does
all this mean?

Do we turn into
scientists every
time we write or
design a page?

What's 700ms
between friends?

Add loads of 700ms delays to every page. Add emotion. Add a light-emitting device, lack of time, children wanting the reader's attention, add any of life's distractions... The question isn't how much it detracts – the question should be why would you do that to your reader when there is another, more respectful way of doing it?

If you respect your readers, you will make the content work for them.

Don't force readers to work your way.

Work theirs.

Content discovery and research

Discovery is an important process.

It's a phase of asking questions and getting answers.

It helps you ensure that when you move to the next phase,

(usually building a prototype, often called an "alpha")

you're moving in the right direction.

It means you're working on data, not guesswork and hunches.

Often, a discovery involves a group of people working together in a room on a specific problem.

It's about open, honest discussion. It usually means a lot of making notes and sketches and talking out loud, and not a lot of peering at computers.

The idea is to get a really good understanding of the nature of the problem – not to start designing solutions.

It's collaborative thinking-out-loud. It's usually quite fun.

Discovery is really important, because it helps you understand:

You can apply discovery to whole sections
of content, or single items.

- your audience
- what your organisation thinks it wants
- what your organisation actually needs
- when you should publish what
- what channels you should use to communicate to whom (and when)
- why you should have a digital team at all

Squishy humans

You can also use discovery to help others in the organisation understand what you are doing and why. This is particularly helpful when dealing with people who have sign-off. I've found the best way of getting people to sign off content with the minimum of fuss is to bring them on the journey with me. I haven't always done this. Sometimes I've had a deadline and I've stormed ahead – I had a 'you can come with me or get out of my way' sort of attitude. But that's not always the best way of doing it.

Using discovery to bring people with you

I work with organisations around the world. In many places the process is like this:

- author writes
- editor edits
- the content goes to be signed off
- it disappears for weeks and both author and editor have to chase several times
- when it comes back, it's been rewritten, and neither author nor editor like it
- it's rewritten and goes around and around like

that for a while
- someone forces the decision to publish
- everyone is unhappy with what is left

Sound familiar?

Content discovery helps you avoid that.

It's a chance for everyone to be involved early on. It's not a guaranteed way of avoiding confrontation and disagreement, but in my experience it helps a great deal.

Making the content journey with people instead of against them can be easier.

How to do a content discovery

The point of discovery is that it's a chance for everyone to share what they know with everyone else. All the participants end up with the same understanding of the problem. Everyone can see the same data.

You know when your discovery is over when everyone who needs to agrees on what the next steps should be.

A good discovery means getting all the right people in one room at the same time. Sometimes you might need just 3 or 4 people for 2 or 3 hours. Other times, you might need 12 people for 2 days. The important thing is to have all the right people in the same place, at the same time. Invite everyone who has an interest in the content you want to work on. Invite writers, editors, designers, developers, delivery and product managers, people with sign-off, and experts from outside the team too.

Conversation with experts

Having experts in the room during discovery gives you a chance to find out the most important things that matter to them, and see how those things fit with the online behaviour you have observed during your earlier research.

If conversation is hard, you can introduce a piece of evidence in a high-level way and then ask if their experience is the same. Always ask open-ended questions at this stage – you are likely to find the answers much more useful.

Conversation with experts can help you find out about:
- Any offline behaviour you haven't seen: experts have anecdotes as well as hard evidence – you should look at both. If your experts are asked the same thing over and over at parties, it's either just

a conversation starter (their happy nature is very attractive) or they have a targeted view of what people think. You'll have to take decisions on what you will use and what you won't.

- Things your experts find themselves constantly repeating: if the experts have to say something over and over again, the answers they're giving must be things people want to know.

Top tips for running a discovery session

- book a big room
- plan the day – include breaks so that people can keep their minds fresh
- stand up as much as possible, keep the atmosphere lively
- make sure there are lots of whiteboards, pens and sticky notes
- ask open-ended questions.
- bring snacks

After discovery

You'll probably end up with a stack of notes and sketches. Work through them as soon as possible after the discovery itself, while your mind is still fresh.

Try to create some sort of mind map, something visual. Put it up on the wall so you can keep it in mind while working (and so your colleagues can all see it too).

Send an email round to all the participants, thanking them for their time and summing up what the team concluded. This is especially helpful to make sure you've understood everything the experts said, and be sure you didn't misinterpret anything.

By the end of your discovery you will have:
- your online audience's view
- your experts' views
- some idea of missing information (this will have come from your experts' anecdotes)
- your organisation's current view (your current info or business goals if you have them)

Finding your audience through research

People who are new to web publishing tend to think their audience are out there, patiently waiting for someone to write something that will interest them. Too often, they assume that all they need to do is put something online and it will be findable, and found, by the right people. It doesn't work like that.

If you want your content to succeed, you need to find your audience. You have to understand:

- who your audience really are
- what they want from you
- and how to speak to them

... before you write a single word.

Your audience are humans

In the old days, when good search engines (particularly Google) were still the new exciting things on the web, people used to do what's called keyword stuffing (putting a lot of keywords on a page, sometimes many times). The search engines would pick up those words, assume that page was more relevant, and push it up the rankings.

Today that sort of behaviour will get you blacklisted (disregarded) by search engines very quickly. If there's one thing the makers of search engines don't like, it's people trying to game the system. So they've made it very hard to do that. Successful content doesn't even try to game the system; it wins by just being good content.

So you need to write your content for humans, not search engines. Good content and natural language will get you further up the rankings than any attempt at trickery. (There's one exception: paid-for advertisements, but that's beyond the scope of this book. There's stacks of information out there on how to make the most of your keyword budget. Before you run off and buy a load of them, remember: humans are often sceptical of ads and will usually just go to the first search result that's clearly not an advert.)

Of course, you know your product or service, and you know your organisation. Does that mean you automatically know what to say to your audience? Maybe. But maybe not.

The thing with prior knowledge is that it colours your judgement.

Who are you talking to? Who do you really want to come

to your site? How well do you really know them? For some people you'll know this. For others, you'll think you know this.

If you've worked in your organisation for a while, you'll have a good measure of who those humans are. But don't forget that people change their habits along with the technology they use. Do you really know your audience as of right now – or as of a few years ago?

If you are new to an organisation, then so much the better. You don't have any preconceived ideas. Don't let this be daunting. It can be a plus, not a minus.

The best way to get to know your audience is to have user researcher on the team. User researchers are professionals whose entire job is to really understand users, and to help the rest of the team understand what needs those users have. They will do this through lots of different research techniques including interviews, surveys and analysis.

Not all organisations see the value in this kind of research, and some don't want to pay someone to do it. If you are in this position, you can still do some desk research to better understand your users. It's not as good as having a user researcher, but it's better than doing nothing.

Introducing Nice Green Energy

All the way through this book, we are going to pretend you are a content person working for a UK-based company called Nice Green Energy. Not everything works the way you'd like it to (because in most organisations, that's what happens).

You're working in a team of 4 content designers based in one office, working alongside the web team. Your marketing and brand team are based in another office about 100 miles away. You have to work with them on all your digital content, but you don't see them often. They have sign-off control, you don't.

Throughout the book, we're going to frame content design problems using examples from Nice Green Energy. That way, you can see the process as it moves from one step to the next, and see how different parts of the process relate to one another.

Finding your audience's vocabulary

The words you use inside your organisation aren't always the same as the words that people outside it would use to describe the same thing. Task number one is to find out what vocabulary your audience is using.

As a content designer at Nice Green Energy, you have been asked to look at a section of the company website that deals with hydraulic fracturing (bear with me here).

The page is failing on your website – traffic data shows that no one visits it, even though the subject is always in the news, and your company (alongside many others in the sector) has been attacked by the media for your policy on hydraulic fracturing.

So what do you do?

You could start with the people in the company who know most about it and get a brief from them. For example, many companies have brand guidelines that will tell you who the audience is and what they are coming to you for. Sometimes these guidelines are based in research, sometimes they are not. The latter is quite dangerous for you as a content designer. If there's no insight leading you to your style, tone of voice and intended audience, you may find that no matter how hard you try, your content fails. Mostly because it will be doing what the organisation wants, and not what your audience wants.

So first of all, find what your audience is saying with some desk research. You can get a stack of research done without moving too far from your actual desk.

Search data

Search data means the words people type into a search engine to get information on the web. 'External' search data refers to trends from places like Google, while 'internal' search data refers to what users enter into the search bar on your website.

External searches happen on other people's websites, and bring users to yours; internal searches happen on your website, conducted by users who have already found it.

Here, we're focusing on external data, because it tells us how users seek information before they come to you, so you can do a better job attracting them. When looking into this for the first time, don't start with internal data – go external, where your audience is. They have all the answers you need right now.

Google Trends will help you find some of the language you are looking for.

Google hides a lot of data and if your audience chooses to search privately or incognito, you won't find all the data you are looking for. However, you will be able to make a very good start.

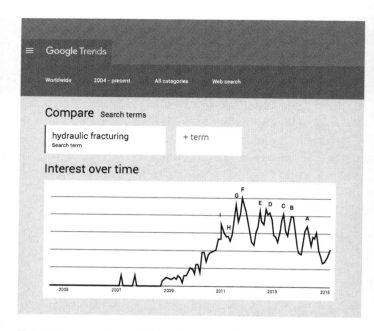

You might start by putting 'hydraulic frac-turing' into Google Trends, which would get you something like this.

There's some traffic – but on closer inspection, you can see it's from 2004 and it's for the entire world. You only care about the UK right now. So let's add filters for UK-only and the last month.

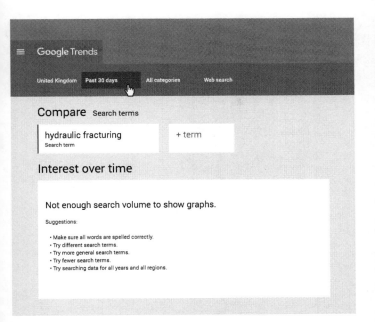

There are so few searches now that nothing's showing up. Maybe that's why people aren't finding your page of information. So let's back up a bit. Let's look over the last year.

Case study

Now it's clear: in Oct 2015, the term 'hydraulic fracturing' completely dropped off the chart. It's so low, Google isn't tracking it now.

Case study

Looking at the media coverage, you keep seeing the word 'fracking'. So let's add that.

Now that's interesting. Compared with 'hydraulic fracturing', 'fracking' is so much higher that 'hydraulic fracturing' doesn't even register.

That might be why the page is failing.

Case study

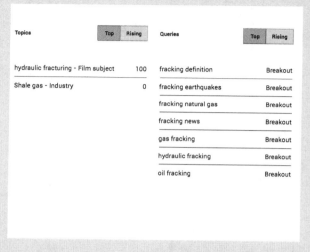

Related searches

Topics			Queries		
	Top	Rising		**Top**	Rising
hydraulic fracturing - Film subject		100	fracking definition		Breakout
Shale gas - Industry		0	fracking earthquakes		Breakout
			fracking natural gas		Breakout
			fracking news		Breakout
			gas fracking		Breakout
			hydraulic fracking		Breakout
			oil fracking		Breakout

Further down this page, you can see related terms people are searching for.

This can give you an idea of what people really want to know and help you narrow your content (if you want to).

Case study

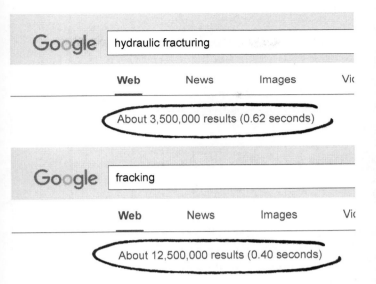

To be honest, you don't even need to go that far sometimes. You can just do a quick search to see what people are writing about the most.

I wouldn't just take this number in isolation and make big content decisions on it, but it is a good indication of the vocabulary other people are using.

Case study

It's pretty clear that more people use 'fracking' than 'hydraulic fracturing', but the page on your website doesn't use the word 'fracking' at all. No wonder no one reads it. No one can find it. Your audience is using a different vocabulary.

This is just one way to find the words your audience is using. There are a number of tools, free and paid for, that can help you with this kind of research; and this type of research can be used for a number of different reasons that we'll get to later in the book. Right now, we're just going to assume you now know what kind of language your audience uses to find this topic. Now you can go out and find them. The more you know about your audience, the more successful you will be.

Using website analytics and metrics

Now you know some of the vocabulary your audience is using, you can find out more about them. This will give you:

- more vocabulary (which can help them find your information)
- what your readers want to know most (so you can prioritise what you publish first)
- their mental models (this is how your audience thinks, which can help you with journeys around your site)

If you already have a website, you can use existing statistics and metrics. You might be able to see:

- how many people visit a page
- how quickly people leave
- most popular links on the page
- time people spend on a page
- search terms used on that page
- where they came from (referrals)
- where they go to

You might already have insight and research, so you might want to skip the rest of this chapter. If you don't have that kind of information, or you haven't interpreted that sort of data before, try some of this.

Referrals

You might want to know where on the web most

of your audience comes from, so that you know where to position your marketing efforts.

You can find this out from the referrals section of Google Analytics or whatever software you use to track your site's traffic. It's also a good way to see where your users come from so you can see what kind of people they are, what they are reading, what language they used to get to your site, what link text they followed to get to you, and more. All of that adds up to more language you can use on the page to engage them.

Number of people visiting a page

There will be 2 metrics here, confusingly called **unique visits** and **visits**:

- unique visits is the number of actual visitors to a page
- visits counts the amount of times that a page is displayed, no matter how many individual people visit. It includes the number of times the page has been reloaded or refreshed in the same browser

For example, your analytics data could show 400 visits, but if they are all just you checking out your own website, that's one unique visit.

Again, you need to be careful with this sort of analysis. If a page only has 5 unique visits a month, you might decide it's time to delete it; but first of all, find out why the page is failing. If you changed the language on the page, would it perform better?

Bounce rate

The term **bounce rate** means slightly different things to different people. It can mean someone landing on a page, not clicking on any of the links and leaving. Some count a bounce as someone arriving at a page and leaving in under 10 seconds. When looking at your data, bounce rates can help you spot pages that aren't working effectively. Be careful though – sometimes, a high bounce rate means a page is working well.

Home > Working, jobs and pensions > Holidays, time off, sick leave, maternity and paternity leave

UK bank holidays

England and Wales   Scotland   Northern Ireland

The next bank holiday in England and Wales is

28 August

Summer bank holiday

 Add bank holidays for England and Wales to your calendar (ICS, 10KB)

Upcoming bank holidays in England and Wales

2017

28 August	Monday	Summer bank holiday
25 December	Monday	Christmas Day
26 December	Tuesday	Boxing Day

2018

1 January	Monday	New Year's Day
30 March	Friday	Good Friday
2 April	Monday	Easter Monday
7 May	Monday	Early May bank holiday
28 May	Monday	Spring bank holiday
27 August	Monday	Summer bank holiday
25 December	Tuesday	Christmas Day
26 December	Wednesday	Boxing Day

If a bank holiday is on a weekend, a 'substitute' weekday becomes a bank holiday, normally the following Monday.

Ho
lea
pa

Hol
Mo

El:
Sc

A successful page meets a need

Here's an example from GOV.UK. When it comes to bank holidays in the UK, most people just want to know when the next one is. So it was put in large, highlighted text in the middle of the page. The other dates are there but not as prominent. People could read it in seconds, and leave. That could be termed a bounce and seen as a bad thing, but in this case the page is doing exactly the job it was meant to. If people spend less than 5 seconds on this page, that's seen as an achievement, not a failure.

Time on a page

This refers to how long a particular reader spends on a particular page. It might be seconds, or minutes. Like the bounce rate, you'll have to make an editorial judgement on whether time on a page is successful or not based on what the page is trying to do. If it's a page with a lot of text that you want people to read, then higher time numbers are a good thing. On the other hand, if it's a page with a single call to action that most people should skip through very quickly, high numbers are a warning sign that something on the page doesn't make sense to them.

Set your success criteria based on the page type or format and subjects you are writing about, not the site as a whole.

Searches on the page

We've talked about searches from a search engine but on-page and in-site searches can be a gold mine of information. If you have a page on hydraulic fracturing and your audience spend little time on that page, but there are lots of searches starting on that page for 'fracking', you can see what's wrong.

If people arrived at your website by clicking a link from elsewhere, what text was linked on that other page? If they came via a search engine then bounced out again, what did they search for that they didn't find on your page? How can you improve your content and their experience?

All this adds up to a list of words you want to use.

How your audience thinks (and searches)

Some people search the web using different words from the ones they would say out loud. Some people talk online in a slightly different way again. You need to look at all that language and make a decision.

It's part of your job to be respectfully nosey about the words your audience uses to refer to your product or service.

The best way I have found to see into the lives of my audience without leaving my desk is to use forums. Forums are little worlds full of users and their vocabulary. You need to find a few to see what humans really think about a subject. Forums can be influenced by a certain way of thinking so, if possible, look at a range of them if you want a good overall view of your audience.

In our example, you could search for 'fracking forum' to get to your microworld of interesting people. At the time of writing, there are over 2 million results for that term on Google. Some of the forums will be very technical, intended for and used by specialists. Some will be for beginners who are just curious, and some will be for everybody. So where to start?

Get a list of what you actually need

A forum can be like a rabbit warren. Go in with a few ideas of what you want out of it. You could set out to find:

- all the types of vocabulary people use to discuss fracking
- the top 10 things your audience wants to know when it comes to fracking
- how emotive this subject is (and who it affects the most)

This will give you:

- a prioritised list of content
- what words to put on the page
- an indication of your style and tone (if you don't already have one for your site)

Remember, this is just a starting point. You'll validate all this later as you move further through the process.

All the types of fracking vocabulary

I looked at 7 forums for this. The most interesting thing I found was that the forum **owners** tended to write in technical jargon and had a formal, knowledgeable tone. The forum **users** used plain language and were very passionate about the subject.

Digital language and spoken language

The way we speak to each other and the way we search digitally can be poles apart. We use body language and tone of voice to convey meaning when we're in front of someone. In person, we rely on other communication cues, so when we search we don't bother with all that.

Many confident web users will type the bare minimum to get what they want from a search engine. But they wouldn't dream of speaking that way. Out loud they'd say: 'Let's take a look at the weather forecast to see if we need a coat today.' But all they'd type into a search engine would be: 'weather london'.

And with the advent of speech recognition technology, we need to think again. For example, people just need to ask Apple's Siri: 'Do I need an umbrella today?' and it will work out what the weather is in the local area and respond appropriately ('Yes, we will see some rain today.').

The trick is to look for patterns. You'll see duplication all over the place. Those duplicated words are your keywords. In the scenario above, the common factor is weather. That's your term. You will need to put the location on the page for people coming to a site and those talking to electronic helpers. Those words are your basics – your building blocks for the rest of the page.

Find out what words your users use

I was part of a team working on information for a British benefit that includes something called 'mandatory reconsideration' as part of the application process. (It's for when a claim has been turned down, at which point the claimant can go back to the government and ask it to review the case).

In user research, one of our participants

(people who had or were going to claim this benefit) spoke at length about the process and said: 'We can do that appeal thingy. I want to do that.' Then she turned back to the computer and typed in 'mandatory reconsideration'. In speech, she hadn't mentioned that term once. And in the application process, an appeal is officially something quite different. But she knew the government would call it 'mandatory reconsideration' so typed it in.

That's why you have to go to different forums and any other places your audience is: to see what they will type. Voice commands are used but not nearly so much as typing (at the moment). So for now, take note of their **digital language**.

The main things people want to know about fracking

Going back to our fracking example from Nice

Green Energy, I can see from forums that the main things people talk about are:

- the effect on the planet
- where fracking will occur ('Is it near me?')
- actions people can take (write to an MP, campaigning opportunities)
- whether fracking is actually a real concern
- fracking and politics

Let's stop there for now. This is our list of prioritised content for Nice Green Energy.

How emotional people are

Some people are far more confrontational online because they'll probably never meet the person they are talking to. Many people wouldn't speak in that way if the person was standing in front of them. You need to keep this in mind while deciding what tone of voice to write in.

Looking at forums, you would see that people are remarkably passionate about fracking. The right response isn't to be over-friendly (in circumstances like this, people would be distrustful of an energy company being too pally). A clear, open tone would be better.

People interested in fracking seem to be open to learning new language, including technical terms, if it will help them understand the problems better. That's going to be helpful in addressing a dual audience (those who are merely curious about fracking, and those who fear their house will fall into a big hole).

Audience demographics

The age, gender and location of an audience can be important for some subjects but these days, they're not as important as they used to be – the internet is squeezing the gap. For the UK in 2015:

- 11% of adults (5.9 million) have never used the internet
- male and female internet usage is almost the same
- main users were aged 15–54, a big age range

Forums won't give you solid-evidence demographical data. You can take a stab in the dark, but it's better to rely on other, formal user research to give you good data here. The thing you can get from forums is an idea of your audience. Fracking seems to attract many different types of people of all ages, but there is a definite voice from householders and those worried about the environmental impact. This means you can tailor your style, tone and sentence length to that audience.

However, fracking can start to affect anyone at any time. The audience is (potentially) changeable, based on news stories that might trigger concern or the location of a new fracking site. Your audience is pretty big and unpredictable. So what do you do?

Narrow it down

Like all companies, Nice Green Energy wants to expand. Ultimately, you really do have every adult homeowner or tenant in the UK in your sights.

That's a lot of vocabulary and a lot of information to wade through. You need to become more targeted.

You are going to prioritise the audience to:
- people who know about fracking and are negative about it (you need to see if you can change their opinion)

- people who don't know about fracking and are negative about it (you need to inform them so they stop spreading inaccurate stories and rumours)
- people who know about fracking and are positive about it (turn them into advocates)
- people who want to know what fracking actually is (so hopefully, they see the positive side and not the negative)

There are many more audiences, but we'll start with these 4.

You have a list of vocabulary in mind, a prioritised set of of concerns you are going to address with your content, and a blank page. It might look something like this:

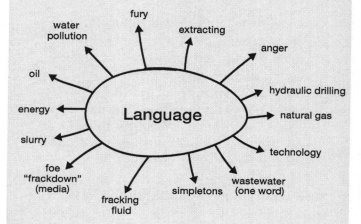

Language

- fury
- extracting
- anger
- hydraulic drilling
- natural gas
- technology
- wastewater (one word)
- simpletons
- fracking fluid
- foe "frackdown" (media)
- slurry
- energy
- oil
- water pollution

Notes:
Really happy to learn new language
Lots of emotion
People argue about spelling a lot

Searches: fracking
(in priority) fracking oil
fracking gas
fracking water
fracking definition → interesting
shale fracking

Priorities: effect on the planet
where (ie is it near me?)
actions people can take
is fracking an actual concern?
fracking and politics

Your research has told you that:
- people use 'fracking', not 'hydraulic fracturing' (but are willing to learn new language)
- the top searches you should provide content for are, in order of priority: fracking, fracking oil, fracking gas, fracking water, fracking definition, shale fracking

Your audience's main priorities are:
- where fracking will occur ('is it near me?')
- the effect on the planet
- actions they can take (write to an MP, campaigning opportunities)

The audience is usually:
- people who live near fracking sites
- people worried about environment
- people who want to do something about it (not everyone worried will want to do anything)

Assumptions and concerns:
1. people who are OK with fracking may not be as vocal as those who hate it
2. you need to decide what you are going to say as the effect on the planet is not just Nice Green Energy's responsibility
3. you need to take into account nearby fracking sites that are not run by Nice Green Energy – you want to distance yourselves if they have dodgy practices

Doing discovery and research means you are better informed and better equipped to start tackling the content design problem.

But there's still a lot more to do before you start actually designing any content.

The next step is writing user stories and job stories.

User stories and job stories

A user story is a way of pinning down what the team need to do

...without telling them how to do it.

A user story looks like this:

<u>As</u> a [person in a particular role]

<u>I want</u> to [perform an action or find something out]

<u>So that</u> [I can achieve my goal of...]

Some examples:

  <u>As</u> a geologist

     <u>I want</u> access to Nice Green Energy's raw data

        <u>So that</u> I can use it in a study I am completing

  <u>As</u> a concerned citizen who already
knows about fracking

     <u>I want</u> to know if Nice Green Energy
is using fracking

        <u>So that</u> I can contact them directly and
tell them to stop

  <u>As</u> a householder living near a proposed fracking site

     <u>I want</u> to know what effect fracking has on
nearby households

        <u>So that</u> I can make a decision
about moving home

**You can see that all these scenarios would
result in very different content, with a different
tone, style, vocabulary and focus.**

The geologist in the example might just need the data. They might not want much in the way of prose at all. After all, they are going to make up their own mind about what Nice Green Energy is doing – they just need raw data. That would be no good at all for the citizen who wants a general introduction to the subject.

User stories are great if you have a number of different audiences who might all want to consume your content. But there's an alternative to user stories that might be better if you only have one audience, and that's job stories.

Job stories are for specific tasks and usually when you have one audience.

They are good for targeted actions.

Job stories
always start with:

When [there's a
particular situation]

I want to [perform
an action or find
something out]

So I can [achieve
my goal of...]

An example job story:

> <u>When</u> I am writing a report about fracking
> <u>I want to</u> get as much data as possible
> <u>So I can</u> write a comprehensive report

This story could apply equally to an expert geologist or to a student of geology. In this instance, it's the task that is more important.

<u>When</u> I want to know if a company is using fracking
<u>I want to</u> find the contact details quickly
<u>So I can</u> contact them in the way I'd prefer

Again, it doesn't matter who you are, it depends how you get the job done.

Lastly:
<u>When</u> I hear fracking is proposed near where I live
<u>I want to</u> know if it is true
<u>So I can</u> decide what, if anything,
I am going to do

It doesn't really matter whether the user here is a homeowner or tenant, or whether they live at that address permanently or temporarily. What matters is whether they are going to be affected by fracking activity.

User stories or job stories

Different organisations use different story methods. These days, I prefer job stories (I am fickle). I find humans change their behaviour a great deal, and job stories cope better with that. Sometimes, user stories can be too wide. Job stories are tidier – they offer more granularity and treat humans as a whole.

Job stories are a better choice if you only have one audience to deal with. You know you need to switch from user stories to job stories if every single user story you write begins with the same thing. If you're writing 'As a shopper, I...' at the beginning of every user story, switch to job stories.

If you have multiple audiences, each of which has different needs for different kinds of content and different levels of detail, you may find user stories better.

How to write a useful job story

Start with something like:
<u>When</u> I am concerned about the effect fracking will have on the planet
<u>I want to</u> find contact details of each company responsible, quickly and easily

<u>So</u> I can contact them directly

**This is an interesting one. But there are actually
two tasks here:**
1. **find out if Nice Green Energy is responsible**
2. **contact Nice Green Energy because they
   are responsible**

So the job story becomes two stories:
<u>When</u> I am concerned about the effect fracking will
have on the planet
<u>I want to</u> find out who is responsible
<u>So</u> I can contact the right organisation

and
<u>When</u> I am concerned about the effect Nice Green
Energy's fracking will have on the planet
<u>I want to</u> find out contact details
<u>So</u> I can complain

**A point to note on this one: some organisations
don't want to make contact easy. Some don't want
their audience to engage – which in the digital age is
madness. Users will find your contact details even if
you don't provide them. So make your contact details
easy to find – you'll frustrate your users less. However,
you may have to deal with this sort of thinking from
others in your organisation.**

Narrowing it down
<u>When</u> I find out fracking might happen near me

> I want to find out exactly where and when
> So I can decide what I am going to do

What if Nice Green Energy is not fracking near someone's house, but another energy company is?

The audience doesn't care who is doing the fracking, only that it is happening. So now you have a clash. Your organisation only wants to talk about its own fracking sites. The audience wants to know about any fracking that affects them. What are you going to do?

Start by narrowing it down:
> When I find out Nice Green Energy's fracking
> might happen near me
> I want to find out exactly where and when
> So I can decide what I am going to do next

This one is similar to the one above but the first one assumes you want to complain. Some people might be pro-fracking and some might just want to move quickly. Without research, we can't work out what their next task is, so we need to keep it quite wide.

Stories often evolve. The first one you write may not be the one you end up with.
> When I want to find out about fracking
> I want to find out the facts from the fiction
> So I can make an informed judgement about it

You'll note there is a theme here. Most of these stories are about taking some action or other. Content usually

results in some sort of action, even if it is just peace of mind or curiosity is sated.

The best content knows it has a purpose and fulfils that purpose. If it doesn't, that content is a waste of space.

This one could lead to action or inaction. For example, if the law is watertight, you can't do anything about it so you might want to move home or vote differently. If the government is saying conflicting things, you could take advantage of that and be very vocal in the discussion. Maybe you can sway things. As a content person, you need to take a view and stand by it.

<u>When</u> I want to find out what the government is saying about fracking

<u>I want to</u> see all the latest, relevant information easily and quickly

<u>So</u> I know what the legal and political position is

Acceptance criteria

Some teams find having acceptance criteria useful. They are short lists of points that indicate that the work on a particular user story or job story is done.

They can be really useful when you have many stake-holders watching your progress, or when you need to keep your team on track through a big and complicated content project.

Meeting acceptance criteria gives your team a chance to tick things off the to-do list.

For:
> <u>When</u> I find out fracking might happen near me
> > <u>I want to</u> find out exactly where
> > > <u>So</u> I can decide what I am going to do

your acceptance criterion might be:
> This story is done when I can find where the nearest fracking site is to the location I am interested in.

Note that the criterion isn't:
> This story is done when I can put in my postcode and see the nearest fracking site.

That puts a solution up front. That's a bad idea. Your audience will tell you what the solution is. Don't assume from the outset that a particular tool (like a postcode look-up) will do the job. If there were only 5 fracking sites in the UK, it would be easier to just publish a list of affected towns and postcodes.

So far, you've done your research and discovery work, and written some stories.

In many organisations, you'll need to get sign-off from above before you can go much further. So let's look at how to get that.

Bringing your organisation with you

I've found the best way to get the rest of an organisation to agree with my work and approach is to run a workshop where all the right people are together.

My advice is to invite anyone and everyone who might influence, stop or change your content.

Get the fact-checkers, the lawyers, the bosses – anyone who might feel the need to interfere.

The Nice Green Energy invitation
list would include:
- the science and environment experts
- the lawyer who has control of final sign-off
- the boss who wants this done quickly
- the head of marketing and brand

Note: I am deliberately making this difficult
because I want to show different techniques.
It's also important to acknowledge that a
significant part of a content designer's job can
be negotiation and persuasion.

You invite all these people because:
- they have to sign off your content
- you'll spend loads of time working with all of them to get anything published
- if you get them all together in one room now, you won't have to have the same conversation multiple times

Sometimes it can be hard to get all those people together, especially if they're senior people. I have some ideas to deal with that.

Make it sound important (because it is)

Don't call it a meeting. Sometimes, a word like 'workshop' does the job, but it is overused and can mean different things to different people.

At Nice Green Energy, you call it a 'decision-making session'.

This will stand out in people's email inboxes. It sounds final and it has an action attached. People in places of authority or responsibility either love, or are scared of decisions. Either way, you probably have their attention.

It also sends a clear message to those people. They:
- are expected to make a decision
- may feel they'll miss something important if they are not there
- are much more likely to open that email

Get people used to the concept

You may need to take time to explain to colleagues how

content decisions are made. Take potentially difficult people out for coffee and go over it with them. Make sure that when the time comes, the idea of a content decision-making session isn't completely new and alien to everyone. You don't want to waste half of the session explaining what it's for and how it works.

Make the purpose clear

Let's meet some of your colleagues at
Nice Green Energy:

- Sandra, the lawyer and a senior decision-maker
- Alan, an expert in environmental matters
- Sam, an expert in fracking

In your invitation, make it clear that the session will result in a decision. That's what the session is for.

Suggest to senior people that if they can't attend, they should delegate someone else to attend on their behalf – someone who has been given the same decision-making power.

When writing your invitation emails, make them powerful. Open with show-stopping facts, if you can. Some examples might be:

Dear Sandra,
There have been 1,032 articles about fracking in the

press in the past month. We have appeared negatively in over 90% of them.

or

Dear Sandra,
82% of our audience rate us highly for satisfaction and we have a 12% increase in sales in the past month. We think we can do better.

or

Dear Sandra,
In recent research, our audience said we are:
- dry and dusty
- boring
- out of date
- inaccurate
- lazy

We need to change this.

Most of the time, leading with a fact can get you positive attention quickly. If it's an insight that has led to the change, include it to give some context – but use it in an action-orientated way.

Make the plan clear

Tell your invitees what the plan is:
Subject: Decision-making session on fracking

Dear Sandra,

There have been 1,032 articles about fracking in the press in the past month. We have appeared negatively in over 90% of them. We need to change this.

The approach

We would like to meet with you, Alan and Sam on: Monday 24 Feb, 10–10.45am, Boardroom A. During this session, we will sign off the content structure for the new fracking content.

Meetings don't always have to be an hour. Make them an odd time – it can focus the mind. I've found people are far more time-conscious if a meeting is 45 minutes long.

Your decision

In this session we, as a group, will decide:

- the content we will cover
- main messages
- channels

If you can't attend, can you send someone else who has decision-making capability?

You are saying, quite clearly and politely, that a decision will be made during this session, with or without their presence.

Preparation

We'll bring:

- details of the content our customers are looking for from us and on this topic in general
- customer journeys (which pages our customers are visiting and where they go)

- a list of vocabulary our customers use to find us

Could you please bring:

- your thoughts on any legal challenges
  we may encounter
- any changes to fracking law we need to cover

What to do in the decision-making session

Welcome everyone to the session.

Tell them its purpose – the goal is to get all of them to agree on:

- a set of job stories, and the order they should be tackled in
- a skeleton structure of headings and subheadings for the content

Point out to everyone that by running this session now, you are saving yourself and all of them a lot of time and pain later on.

If you had everyone in the discovery phase with you, you can just give a summary. If you didn't, you will have to go into some detail. Start by showing them your research, including:

- analytics

- public perception (if applicable)
- the visuals of your conversations with the experts

Then explain what a user story or job story is and briefly explain why you use them. Then show those too.

The more visual you can make it, the better. Make it all about the content and not about you, your thoughts or your opinions. It is far harder to argue with an inanimate product (like a website) or people who are not there (the website audience).

Try not to position so it looks like you are pushing the decision-makers towards a decision you want. Share your knowledge openly and ask them to contribute; not in a them-and-us way, but in a way that invites them to be equal with you.

This session is for everyone to stop thinking about what team they are in. They need to focus on being a team and aiming for a common goal.

Keep it short. You don't want people to get bored. They need to validate what they say or when they disagree with each other.

When you speak, say things like:
    'Research shows…'
    'Our clients are saying…'
    'When we spoke to you, you said…'

This might sound daft, but remember to smile. Unless

you are very good at it, I wouldn't recommend going into full comedian mode, but if you have a tricky history with the participants of this session, you might come across as too authoritarian, and therefore positioning. Watch your body language – be open, stay calm, smile.

If the reception is frosty and the decision-makers give you a hard time, and if you believe the issue is important enough to risk a possible confrontation, show evidence of the website audience failing at specific tasks, or criticising the product or service.

Video of user research is particularly powerful for this if you have it. Nothing gets to the heart of the problem faster than a real user saying what they really think while trying to use a website.

Remember, each person in the room will have a different view on the same thing and some people may be quieter than others. As a facilitator, you need to make sure you have all the information you need.

Your job is to:
- be the voice of the audience you've researched
- keep everyone focused on the job stories (let your participants show gaps, but if it is not a job story backed by evidence, it doesn't get in)
- make sure all voices in the room are heard, not just the loudest ones

Sometimes, these events are tense. People take a position, try to appear superior, maybe even switch off completely. To get the best out of it, try to detach a bit. See yourself as a facilitator, not a content person. Every time you want to make a statement, phrase it as a question and you might get further.

By the end of this session, you should have on the wall:

- a list of job stories that everyone agrees are important
- ideally, some skeleton content (headings and subheadings)

Top tips for decision-making sessions

- as with discovery, make sure there are plenty of whiteboards, walls, pens and sticky notes
- be a good facilitator: don't allow people to go off on tangents
- book a big room with natural light
- if there's a lot of content to discuss, plan some breaks to keep people's minds fresh
- as each decision gets made, write it on a sticky note and put it on a section of wall marked DONE – this helps people remember what's already been decided, and motivates them to keep going
- at the end, wrap up very briefly with: 'OK, we have decided to do this, this and this.'

Designing content

You've done a lot of preparatory work to get this far, but all of it was essential for the next step:

actually designing content.

Start by thinking about formats

Your user stories have told you that your audience wants to know if fracking is happening near them. You could do that with flat content (just words on a page, perhaps a map; nothing that moves or needs any sort of interaction beyond reading or listening). But wouldn't it be better if you let your audience see a more tailored result?

As we mentioned before, the content design choice you make here depends on how many sites in the UK are affected. If there were only 3 proposed fracking sites in the UK, you could take care of that in a sentence. If there are 3,000, that's a long page of listings.

With your user stories and job stories backing you up, you're now in a position to start proposing solutions. You can say, 'No one will read a list of 3,000 addresses, so let's build a postcode look-up tool.' That's content design, right there. You are designing the content for your audience.

You are not editing anything. You are barely writing anything. But you are **designing content**.

Formats are different ways of presenting information on a page. Text is one format. A postcode look-up tool is another format. Other formats include calculators, or calendars, or maps, and so on. Anything that presents information in some way.

Prioritising

Prioritise the most complicated tasks: anything that needs extra skills will take longer, so get those things started first.

When you are looking at what content to produce first, I would recommend prioritising these things, in this order:
1. anything your research shows users want from you
2. information that limits reputational damage to your organisation
3. things that will need more developer time to build

You'll also need to decide how much you are going to publish. You don't need to publish everything. What you don't publish is as important as what you do publish.

The more you publish, the more you expect your audience to read, and the more you'll have to update and maintain. You're creating more work for everyone.

Turning stories into content

Let's take each of the stories we have.
<u>When</u> I am concerned about the effect fracking will have on the planet
<u>I want to</u> find out if Nice Green Energy is one of them
<u>So</u> I can complain (if appropriate)

This story assumes the user already has a negative view of fracking. Finding out about fracking, and Nice Green Energy's policy on safe fracking are other needs.

The acceptance criterion is:
This story is done when I know if Nice Green Energy has fracking sites.

Nice Green Energy has just 12 fracking sites in the UK. You can put addresses and maps to those and add contact details. You can then do some research about what tasks this might lead to, like the safety of fracking or the benefits of fracking.

Another story:
<u>When</u> I am concerned about the effect Nice Green Energy's fracking will have on the planet
<u>I want to</u> find out contact details
<u>So</u> I can complain

Acceptance criterion:

This story is done when I know how I can complain to Nice Green Energy.

This one is also easy: a simple page with several different routes to complain (phone, email, post).

<u>When</u> I find out Nice Green Energy's fracking might happen near me

<u>I want to</u> find out exactly where and when

<u>So</u> I can decide what I am going to do

Acceptance criterion:

This story is done when I know where Nice Green Energy's fracking will take place.

For this, you're thinking a map with a timetable. We also need to look into providing alerts to the team to change the content when the dates of proposed fracking sites go through their consultation and active stages.

<u>When</u> I find out fracking might happen near me

<u>I want to</u> find out who is responsible

<u>So</u> I can decide what I am going to do next

Acceptance criterion:

This story is done when I know who is responsible for the proposed fracking near me.

You need to be careful with this one: you will be handling other organisations' information. That means it's up to you to make sure the information you provide is up to date. Let's say your organisation has decided

to go ahead with this page. A rival company called
MuckyGen has a fracking site not far away, and you
don't want to get mixed up in their bad publicity.

You'll need a map pulling in all the other energy
companies' data so you can display it with yours, with
as little work as possible. The development and design
teams need to put it on their lists of things to do.

> When I want to find out about fracking
>> I want to find out the facts from the fiction
>>> So I can make an informed judgement about it

Acceptance criterion:
> This story is done when I know what's a myth and
> what the real facts are about how fracking affects the
> environment and my area.

From the forum research work, we know people like
myth-buster articles. There are a lot of scary stories
surrounding fracking, few of which have any basis in
science or fact. So you have decided to create some
content to give people firm facts.

Lastly, you have:
> When I want to find out what the government is
> saying about fracking
>> I want to see all the latest, relevant information
>> easily and quickly
>>> So I know what the legal and
>>> political position is

This is a very large subject and it's not Nice Green

Energy's responsibility to cover it. The government publishes all that information anyway. You might want to link to it, but you don't need to repeat it.

What do you want to control?

You and your organisation need to make a decision on how much you are going to publish and what you want to control.

For example, your desk research showed there is another website that shows fracking locations across the UK on a map. It's easy to understand and presented well. Do you need to have your own version of that?

Sometimes, the answer is yes: if you want to control the messages, you don't trust the other website, or the map is inaccessible or out of date. You don't want to link to a site that might say you are causing environmental damage, or send your readers to a map that displays incorrect site locations. You may end up with your audience having a negative view of your company, because of someone else's content.

Sometimes, you just want to keep users on your site as long as possible so you can give them all the facts as you see them (or encourage purchases if you are retail site, for instance). It wouldn't be beneficial for you to send those users off to another site when they might not come back.

However, if someone is doing it better than you and you don't need to do it, don't bother. Don't try to control things that you don't need to control. Focus on the value you and your organisation can add. Get that right first, and then perhaps come back to the map idea later when you have done more research, come up with a better idea, or realised you can do it in a better way.

Style and tone

If you already have a style guide, then you can get writing. If you don't have one, you can borrow one from elsewhere. The BBC, the Guardian and GOV.UK have all published style guides on the web. If you have time, you can always adapt one of these to suit your needs, or write one from scratch. You can shape your style and tone based on research.

Now

finally

you are ready
to write.

Writing content

Earlier, about securing sign-off, we talked about getting agreement from colleagues and management to basic structure for the content, perhaps even a set of headings and subheadings.

Now's the time to put them to use.

When a page of text is broken up this way, it's easier for readers to take in the information.

They can understand or predict what information is on the page, because the subheadings tell a story.

Headings and subheadings

As a content designer, you are not just putting words on a page because the words work. You are taking your users on a journey. The words are only part of that experience.

Headings are very important

Search engines think that the words you put in headings and titles are really important. If your heading is 'London: top 10 places to visit' you'll probably get higher search engine rankings than if it is 'Visit the party capital of the UK' (and you'll have to put 'London' pretty close to the title – make it the first word in the copy – in case people think it's Manchester, Liverpool or Edinburgh).

Headings are the first thing your audience will see in search results, so make them targeted and relevant. Your headings are what will pull your audience to your site from search or, if your audience is already on your site, it will tell them they are in the right place.

Hilarious headings

Humour is hard on the internet. It's very easy for people

to misinterpret. If you have witty headings, be sure your audience will get the joke or you risk putting off potential clients or annoying your audience. Of course, content marketing will often use vague titles to pull in an audience. You've probably seen a picture with link text saying: 'You'll never believe what happened next!' Don't write like that. There's now research that shows it doesn't work anyway.

The reality is that most users, most of the time, are people on a mission. They have a specific task in mind. They will skip your funny jokes to get to the more meaningful content.

Your tone and style can come out in different ways, and the words and interactions on the page can carry your brand. A heading is a signpost to content.

Front-loading your headings

Think about front-loading your headings. The faster people consume your information (the scientific bit about how people read is in chapter 2), the happier they are, generally.

Front-loading means putting the most important word(s) of the sentence at the beginning. If you front-load your headings, you make it easier and quicker for readers to understand the content.

For example, which of these headings is

quicker to understand?

What are the facts about fracking?

or

Fracking: the facts

The second one's more effective, because it's the one people will understand faster. The earlier the most important words appear, the better.

Another couple of examples:

How to apply for a membership

or

Apply for membership

When will my delivery arrive?

or

Delivery times

Again, the second choices are front-loaded and will be more easily understood.

You can use statements to get to the point or for a more authoritative tone, and you can use them for more casual purposes too:

What to do about bullying

or

Bullying: spot it and stop it

First paragraph

The first paragraph on the page is to orientate the reader – it tells them that they are in the right place and that they will get the information they are looking for.

Your audience has probably followed a search engine result or link somewhere to get to you. The first things people want to know are 'Did I make the right choice?' and 'Do I need to go back and search again or find something else?'

Years ago, when I worked in advertising, I heard there was an old adage that copywriters held in their minds when writing: 'You have 5 seconds to get my attention, and 11 to keep it.' Now, I think it's much shorter.

You probably have 3 seconds to get my attention, and 5 to keep it.

So the first paragraph on a page is very, very important. Make those 3 seconds count.

Headings for pages that just do one thing

If your page just does one thing – perhaps it's a tool, or displays a video – your page title should be specific enough to tell the user exactly what they're getting. If your audience is in a task-completion mode, many will simply skip any text you put at the top of the page anyway.

If you need to interrupt their task-based behaviour, make sure you really have to and that it's pertinent to starting the action.

That said, I have seen this 'ignore all words and get to the action' behaviour on many sites I've worked on. In some circumstances, I have observed all research participants read every single word placed before the tool they were to use. Admittedly, there were just two sentences on that page, but even that surprised me. The point I'm trying to make is: know your audience and test. Just because you think you know what is going to happen, doesn't mean it will.

80/20 rule

So, with your research and your user needs, you know what is important for your audience. With that in mind, you can put what most people are looking for right up front (remember the GOV.UK bank holidays example we looked at in chapter 3). This is the 80/20 rule. Put the information that 80% of your audience is looking for first. The information the other 20% of your audience is looking for should be there – and findable from a search engine – but not front and centre. It will put off 80% of your audience.

Getting rid of users

In content marketing spheres, the thought of getting rid of users is probably a cardinal sin, but with good content design you will respect your users' time. If they are on the wrong page, you will need to get rid of them as soon as possible.

If you are selling an item and the user is on the wrong page, offering an unobtrusive alternative can benefit your organisation. (But never with a pop-up that says 'Are you sure you want to leave?' That's just one of the most annoying things on the web.) A well-placed search box on the page will always offer an alternative if the user thinks they will get what they want.

If you have a task-based information page – say, to apply for something – making sure your audience is eligible to make the application is probably the most important thing. No one wants to waste time on something they definitely can't get. For example, Nice Green Energy's page for school-age children interested in doing work experience might begin with:

Apply for work experience
You are only eligible for work experience at Nice Green Energy if you:

- are over 16
- live within a 10-mile radius of our head office at (address)
- include a scan of a signed letter from your head teacher with your application

Scent of information vs the three-click rule

There's a book called Information Foraging Theory written by Peter L T Pirolli, published in 2007. Despite its age, it's an mine of information that is mostly still relevant today. In short (I'm reducing 216 pages to a sentence here), it says that users will go as far as they need to, and click as many times as they need to, as long as the 'scent of information' is strong.

In other words: as long as a person thinks they will get the information they need, and they don't think they are on the wrong path, they will continue for quite some time.

You can use this for structuring the information on your website, in-page copy, and tools and transactions. As long as you follow your audience's mental model of how the information will be available, and you provide a strong scent of information, you are on the right path.

That's not an excuse to be verbose. What I'm saying is: people don't always abandon a task within a set number of clicks.

Subheadings

Subheadings on a page have a number of different purposes:

- Subheadings tell a story.
  People often look down a page when they land on it to see how long it is and what it is about. Subheadings help you tell your audience in seconds exactly what information they are going to get. Your visitor can then see if they are on the right page and if they should give their time and attention.
- Subheadings break up the text.
  Most people don't want to be greeted with a wall

of text. Most of us will go through it if we want the information, but it automatically makes it seem a little bit harder. Subheadings make the task easier.

- Subheadings help you remember and understand. When you read a very complex or long document, your brain will see subheadings as markers. If you need to go back through the text you have read, it's easier to remember where that info is if there's a subheading nearby (particularly if your subheadings tell a coherent story).

Remember all the vocabulary you found in analytics and in forums? Those words are perfect for headings and subheadings. If people have a word or phrase in mind, they will look for it on the page to make sure they are in the right place. Search engines will regard those terms as important to the content and may rank you higher than someone who has just put a single version of that term on the page somewhere.

Writing and punctuation

Bullet points break things up

In the same way that subheadings break up text, so do lists. It's not a good idea to have an entire page of them – that's hard to read – but bullets can be

great because they:
- can make text quicker to read
- make the page less dense
- can bring out the most important points without adding other design elements that might clutter your page

The way you do bulleted lists is a matter of style. Generally I'd go with: if it has a lead-in sentence, use lowercase at the start of each of the bullet points. If there's no lead-in, uppercase. Punctuation at the end of a sentence is entirely optional. Screen readers (software products designed to help people with visual impairments read digital content) will pause longer if there is a comma at the end of each point. That's about it, though.

Word counts aren't always important

You can be boring in 5 words or fewer. I generally don't follow word counts for that reason. I find people won't keep it short if they think they have space to fill up. Often, especially for task-based pages, the shorter the content, the better.

If you keep to the user need, you'll be interesting and, therefore, engaging.

Different audiences will go to different lengths to get their information and they'll want it in different ways. Some academics love 100,000-word PDFs because they can print them off more easily than some web pages. They print because they like being able to mark up notes on paper, not on screen. The rest of the web world screams 'No PDFs!' (with good reason – they are not very accessible, for example) but if your web pages don't print very well, you can see why people want PDFs, right?

The way to find the correct word count is:
- answer the user need – and only the user need
- don't be boring (aka verbose)
- think how your audience will use the information (this will influence the format it is in)
- respect your audience's time and the environment they are in (this may influence how long they will read for)

Keep sentences short

I'm not the only one who says this.

The Oxford Guide to Plain English recommends 15–20 words per sentence. It also says:

'If you regularly exceed 40 words, you'll certainly weary and deter your readers.'

Jyoti Sanyal, author of Indlish (the book for every English-speaking Indian), said:

'Based on several studies, press associations in the USA have laid down a readability table. Their survey shows readers find sentences of 8 words or less very easy to read; 11 words, easy; 14 words fairly easy; 17 words standard; 21 words fairly difficult; 25 words difficult and 29 words or more, very difficult.'

Author Ann Wylie said:

'When the average sentence length in a piece was fewer than 8 words long, readers understood 100% of the story. At 14 words, they could comprehend more than 90% of the information. But move up to 43-word sentences and comprehension dropped below 10 percent.'

There's a stack of different research out there, but the main point is that long sentences aren't as easy to understand as shorter ones.

Jargon

One person's specialist language is another person's jargon.

There are times when you need to introduce an audience to a new term or phrase. There are other times when you assume everyone knows what you are talking about. However, the magic word there is _assume_.

If you are teaching, you will want to introduce new terms. If you are sharing your knowledge, thoughts or feelings, you might want to introduce new vocabulary. If you want to really share with the world, rather than show off, introduce the term but explain it the first time on the page. It won't hurt. It will definitely help.

There are many reasons not to use jargon (at least without explaining it the first time you use it on the page). Here are some of the main arguments I hear that jargon-busting content designers might have to contend with.

'This is for specialists. Everyone will know what I am talking about.'

That just can't be true. It would suggest that there are never newcomers to that specialism – ever. It would also suggest that there's no one who is just curious about your field of expertise and might want to expand their horizons into your world.

'You are dumbing it down'

This is the sentence I struggle with most. It says the author thinks they are cleverer than the audience they are talking to.

People who are well read (aka not dumb) read a lot. They don't have time to wade through jargon. They want the information quickly and easily – just like everyone else. Wanting to understand quickly has little to do with intelligence. It has a lot to do with time and respect.

Filling web pages with turgid prose doesn't make anyone look clever; it makes them look arrogant and disrespectful. They don't care what people think of the writing or how long it takes the audience to get through it.

> '9-year-olds won't want to read this. Why are you
> writing in that language?'

This argument comes from organisations trying to push a certain reading age.

The average reading age in the UK is about 9 years. The average 9-year-old has over 30,000 terms in their vocabulary. If you cover up 30% of words on a page, a 9-year-old will still be able to accurately guess the content.

Writing **for** an age range isn't the same as writing **to** that age. Most 9-year-olds will not be interested in insurance. But someone who is 49 with little time, or dyslexia, or a small phone screen, or a life to live, will benefit from you getting to the point quickly and with little jargon.

As I said before: it's not dumbing down, it's opening up.

Respecting the audience

If we write clearly with good structure, short sentences and plain language we are helping people read. In the UK alone, this means we may be helping:
- 1.5 million people who have a learning disability
- 7 million (conservative estimate) people who have dyslexia
- 2 million people with a visual impairment
- lots of people using a poor internet connection

- most people who don't want to read and reread something just to understand it

Plain language

Plain language isn't just about not using jargon, it's about using language that is clear to your audience. Take these examples:

> It is a simple fact that continuing to keep regular checks and constantly watching cold water rising in temperature until it arrives at the boiling point of 100 degrees centigrade, will not, in fact, make it come to that perfect temperature any faster than, say, staring at the nearest wallpaper.

> Watching water boil won't make it boil any faster.

See what I mean?

A 9-year-old can read that first example (I know, I tested it on several of them). It's just turgid and not to the point. It uses simple, plain language – but it's not clear. It's not easy to digest the information.

Plain language doesn't mean short and terse, or that the writing will lack atmosphere or feeling either. Try this:

> We listened to the snow fall. You'd think it would be silent but it's not. Not if you really, really listen. There's the gentle thud of each tiny flake falling on its brother or sister, each nestling down for the winter.

That's plain English, written briefly. But it's full of atmosphere and emotion.

Being clear in your language is the fastest route to making someone else understand what you are trying to communicate. Nothing else.

Punctuation

The first point to remember is that most people in the UK don't know how to use little-used punctuation (square brackets, semicolons, etc). Lots of people **can read it** correctly, but they **can't use it** correctly or confidently in adult life. Stick to using familiar punctuation like commas and full stops.

If you have a site that is meant to be easy to understand, make it easy to understand.

Ask yourself what sort of audience you have and what punctuation you should use. I've never seen anyone abandon a page because of a semicolon. But consider the speed your audience is reading at and how you can help them speed up or slow down. You can usually do that really effectively with familiar punctuation.

Just to make this point really, really clear: I am not saying don't use anything but commas and full stops. I use all the punctuation I can get away with, all the time. I love it. But when working on some websites, I know my audience want short sentences they can understand quickly; they don't want to marvel at how well I can wrangle the English language.

Remember, this is not about perceived intelligence – it's about speed of reading and comprehension. Nothing else.

You can also use punctuation to add rhythm to your work. You can emphasise a point by writing in short sentences. Maybe repeat certain words. Or you can add some length to your sentence (remembering the amount of words can influence understanding) and take your audience on a journey.

See what I did in those paragraphs? ;)

Images

A picture paints a thousand words. Well, only if you can see it.

As content designers, we know that sometimes a graphic or icon is a good idea. You are not treading on a designer's toes here (although they may feel that way). This is where you are a content designer and not a writer. If your audience will better understand what you are trying to say with a picture, use one.

For example, if you are telling people to look for a certain logo as a mark of quality, you should show that logo. However, make sure it is accessible. Make sure you have an alternative.

Ask yourself if there's a better way of doing it. If someone is on a train with a poor phone signal, are they going to completely miss the point of your content piece if they can't see all of it? What alternative can you offer? What alt text (alternative text for assistive technologies) will you include?

This is often a good opportunity to work collaboratively with a designer. Together, you can create an image that works for your users and for both of you.

Talking of collaboration: sometimes, writing on your own doesn't work.

You need input from someone else.

That's when you should try pair writing.

Pair writing

Writing content alongside someone else (both of you, at the same time, in front of the same computer or piece of paper) is called pair writing.

Your pair can be anyone: they could be another content designer, a service designer, a subject expert, your lawyer, the receptionist – anyone really.

The point of pair writing is that it gives you double the brain power. It's like getting through both the first and the second draft simultaneously.

The results are powerful, but the experience can be both challenging and productive.

Sometimes fun, but not always.

Pair writing is useful because:

1. you get more work done, faster
2. you can get the content signed off faster (if your pair-writing companion is the person who's responsible for sign-off)

3. your whole
organisation
works more
collaboratively,
which results in
more trust and
better working
relationships
all round

It's hard for one person to write content that's both accurate and easy to read. That's one reason why pair writing is such a good idea. There are always experts in every organisation who know every single detail about how each particular thing works. They can write accurately. But they're not always good at explaining it clearly — precisely because they know too much about it. Their minds are too focused on the detail.

Pair writing helps you get the best out of both brains.

Writing content about fracking

Let's imagine a Nice Green Energy job story that looks like this:

When I find out fracking
might happen near me
I want to find out exactly where
So I can decide what I am going to do

Your team decided this need could be best met using a postcode look-up tool, but it needs some additional content to end with. There's no point leaving your users with a pin on a map and no supporting information.

Remember those Nice Green Energy colleagues we introduced in chapter 5? One of them was Sam, an expert on fracking. She can tell you how far the new fracking site will extend, what effect it will have, what the noise level will be, the lot. She's going to be an ideal pair writing companion. (You already have analytics data that tells you what people are looking for, so you can anticipate the kind of answers they'd want from someone like Sam.)

With Sam's help, you realise that the content needs to address finer-grained user stories, like this:

> <u>When</u> I find out fracking might happen near me
>> <u>I want to</u> find out if that proximity will mean my house will collapse
>>> <u>So</u> I can decide what I am going to do

Sam can tell you exactly what will happen. She wants to explain how deep the fracking goes, why it will or won't cause subsidence and give reassuring advice. Your tone and style says the content should be friendly and reassuring. So how can you do all that and keep to the story?

1. how deep fracking goes is interesting to a whole bunch of audiences, not just people directly affected by it. That's a story in and of itself. You need to decide whether to link to it or feature it.
2. the story doesn't say people want to know why something happens. They just want to know if it will happen to them. While those 2 things can be directly linked, do they need to be on the same page?
3. how do you reassure someone who is af-fected? Will they believe you?

Happily, the answer to the original question

('Does fracking mean my house will collapse?')
is no. There's no risk of subsidence. Well,
there's no evidence of it – which can be a
different thing when people don't trust you.

When writing, you will start with a page that
follows the 80/20 rule (80% of people just want
to know if their house will sink, nothing else).

The content should be something like this:
> Subsidence risk from fracking
> Residents are often worried there's a risk
> of subsidence from fracking. The answer is
> no – there is no risk.
> The reasons why are:
> [You and Sam write three paragraphs
> of good content linking off to deep,
> technical content.]

Sam is happy with that, because it's accurate.
You're happy with it, because it's easy to read.
Two brains, working together.

All the way through your pair-writing
session you have:
- explained why you are suggesting edits:
  Sam is learning about how users consume
  information as much as you are learning about fracking

- listened to Sam's fears closely and questioned her: Sam may want another 50 words on the page and you don't. But when you dig a little deeper, you find it is because she is always asked about that point when talking about this scenario
- learnt about any other needs you may have missed

Writing with other people

Successful pair writing depends on your relationship with your partner and their willingness to do things in a user-centred way. Sometimes, it can take time (perhaps several actual pair-writing sessions) for the 2 of you to build that relationship.

Some pair-writing partners are keen to jump in and really try to help. Others can get argumentative. When that happens, try to understand why. I have often found that it's because no one has explained to my partner how reading behaviour has changed. Or no one has talked to them about their view of language and how online behaviour works. Those people are not trying to be obstructive or difficult, it's just that no one has explained these things to them.

Sometimes, you might encounter people who have antiquated opinions ('Well, that's not what I learned in school') and they don't want to change them. All you can do is be professional and be the voice of the user. Make your case using the research you did earlier in the process, and the insights that came from it.

Other times, the relationship can be tested because your expert partner keeps suggesting things, and you keep saying no because you don't think they're clear enough. It can sour the atmosphere. Try to avoid this by staying positive from the start. Rather than actually saying no, try typing your own suggestions. Keep your tone encouraging and lively. Say: 'Could we put it like this? How about we say that with simpler words like these? We could simplify that in this way.' And so on.

Top tips for pair writing

- find a quiet space for the 2 of you to work together
- write the user story out on paper, and keep it close by so that it's uppermost in your minds throughout
- get a big monitor and bump up the text size, so you can both clearly read every word
- constant experimentation is OK; type something, and ask 'Does this work?'
- try not to work together for more than 2 hours at a time (more than that, and both brains start to lose focus)

OK. You've written some content. Now it's time for a crit.

Crits

'Crit' is a short nickname for content critique

A crit is an opportunity for other people to comment on a piece of content that's been drafted by an individual, or by 2 people doing pair writing.

Usually, it means getting a team of people to sit round a big screen that displays the content. Everyone joins in with their thoughts. One person takes notes.

Crits can be hard to deal with.

It's not easy to let other people tear your hard work to shreds.

It's not easy to listen to them telling you what's wrong with it.

Many people, quite naturally, fear it turning into a slanging match.

That's why crits have rules, so that they become safe environments for meaningful feedback.

The rules are:

- be respectful: everyone did the best job possible with the knowledge they had at the time
- only discuss the content, not the person who created it

- **only give constructive criticism: 'That's crap' is unhelpful and unacceptable**
- **no one has to defend a decision**

Making the environment safe is the most important part of making a crit work. No one likes getting heaps of criticism.

If crits are a new idea in your organisation, it can take a while to get them to work.

If you have introverts in your team, you will need to help them. But stick with it: crits are a very efficient way of getting feedback from many different people all at the same time.

I use crits to:
- establish or iterate a style guide: having the content team around for short periods can move a style guide on faster than a set of meetings

- build a team: invite
  the designers
  and developers,
  so they can see
  exactly what the
  content people are
  producing; over
  time, designs will
  be more relevant
- establish
  or maintain
  consistency
- spark ideas

Why crits are important

This is about a crit that proved its worth.

I started working for an organisation to set up a team working on digital transformation. Half the content team had worked with me before, so settled easily into crits. The others hadn't experienced crits before and were not very happy. They felt it was demeaning and that their skills were being questioned. The designer on the team wanted to get on with the designs and the developer had a tool to develop.

I spent time with the staff explaining that skills were never in question. Crits were just a way we could work together, efficiently, on the product. We were a new team: we needed to learn and improve what we were doing. Long meetings are boring. Talking for short bursts in a crit was a much better way.

The designer and developer were sullen. Crits were for content – why did they have to come? I persuaded them to come anyway.

The first bit of content in the first crit showed why everyone needed to be there. It was a tiny piece of copy that would be used all over the site (about the price of phone calls to certain numbers). The designer needed to come up with a design element to handle that, so we weren't just writing the same sentence 53 times across the site. It got quite complex; the developer said it would be much better to have an in-page calculator. Within 20 minutes, all 3 disciplines (content designers, designers, developers) were talking about the best solution. In the end, the content was much better for it.

After that, there were no more arguments about attending crits.

People realised that if their discipline wasn't represented, they might miss the chance to make the product better.

I learned that you can also use crits to bring others in the organisation with you. Inviting experts to a crit is the same as inviting them to a discovery session – you can get all their knowledge faster, so you can get to the end product faster.

Subsidence content crit at Nice Green Energy

The pair-writing exercise was a success, so now it's time to put that content through a crit. It's time to invite Sandra (the lawyer and senior decision-maker) and a new colleague called Nathan, who's in charge of communications and branding, to join in. Nathan is going to get the comms backlash (if there is any) and Sandra has final sign-off.

The copy you created while pair writing was:
Subsidence risk from fracking
Residents are often worried there's a risk of subsidence from fracking. The answer is no – there is no risk.

Nathan's OK with this, but Sandra's not happy. She doesn't want to open with a negative. Also, legally, she doesn't feel you can say the risk doesn't exist. It will open Nice Green Energy to criticism if it ever comes to light that there is an instance of subsidence.

Sandra wants this instead:

> Subsidence risk from fracking
> Some residents can be slightly worried there's a risk of subsidence from fracking. At the moment, there is no evidence of a risk.

Here, you've changed the sentence to 'some' and 'slightly worried' but while this makes it less negative, it sounds like we are trying to make light of some people's fears. You know from research that your audience likes myth-busters. You need to face the myth head-on and deal with it.

> **Subsidence risk from fracking**
> Some residents can be worried there's a risk of subsidence from fracking but there's no evidence that's true. Drilling happens deep underground and is only 6–9 inches in diameter, so disruption is kept to a minimum.
> Sources of evidence:
> - the Association of British Insurers <u>released evidence in 2016 to say there is no risk</u>.
> - the respected academic George Respectworthy, who has 50 years' experience in fracking, released a report: <u>'Shale gas: why your house won't collapse'</u>

Here, you are providing evidence instead of saying there isn't any. You are showing your audience something, not telling them. By trusting humans to make up their own minds, you are respecting their intelligence. They won't mind that and they are more likely to trust you.

Everyone likes that option. Sandra is able to sign it off on the spot. That means the copy can go straight into the content management system for proofreading and publishing.

Now you just need to track that content, iterate when necessary and have a well-earned cup of tea. Before you go and do it all again, on another piece of content.

Top tips for crits

- there's no set rule for how often you do crits; adjust the frequency to suit your workload and the rhythm of the team
- doing a crit early in the process stops people getting too attached to their copy before it's improved, and helps everyone be confident that they're heading in the right direction
- you don't have to wait until after pair writing – you can do a crit at any stage of the process
- take turns to be the note-taker
- crit is short for critique, not criticism. If content designers end up defending their work, the environment is wrong. Keep the crit focused on making the product better
- content designers don't have to take all the suggestions given in a crit. There needs to be trust from senior management that the content design team know what they're doing, and trust between content designers to do the right thing

Finished pages

One of our job stories was:
> <u>When</u> I am concerned about the effect Nice Green
> Energy's fracking will have on the planet
>> <u>I want to</u> find out contact details
>>> <u>So I can</u> complain

Acceptance criterion:
> This story is done when I know how I can
> complain to Nice Green Energy.

**You can see we have put digital first.
We want people to use the digital
channel as much as possible. By
making email the top option, we
are hoping to make that the easiest
route for people.**

Search

Get in touch

Home > Get in touch

If you want to talk to us, we would love to hear from you.

Email
customerservice@BGE.com
We aim to get back to you within 5 working days.

Post
**Nice Green Energy
Big Field One
Left of the Farm
Fieldsville
AB1 2DE
United Kingdom**
We aim to get back to you within 7 working days.

Telephone
0300 111 222 333
We're open 9–5, Monday to Friday.

NGE ____ Home   Our tariffs   News   Login

Our second job story was:

<u>When</u> I find out Nice Green Energy's fracking might happen near me

<u>I want to</u> find out exactly where and when

<u>So I can</u> decide what I am going to do

Acceptance criterion:

This story is done when I know where Nice Green Energy's fracking will take place.

For this, we're thinking a map with a timetable.

Fracking timetable

Search

NICE GREEN ENERGY

Home > News > Fracking timetable

	Area	Date
1	Abbey Fields	September 2016
2	Brockenwocken	October 2017
3	Chippersville	November 2018
4	Devendslowe	December 2019

NGE   Home   Our tariffs   News   Login

Our third job story was:

<u>When</u> I find out fracking might happen near me
<u>I want to</u> find out who is responsible
<u>So I can</u> decide what I am
going to do next

Acceptance criterion:

This story is done when I know who is
responsible for the proposed fracking near me.

We need a map pulling in all the other
energy companies' data so we can
display it with ours, with as little work
from us as possible. The development
and design teams need to put it on their
list of things to do.

Fracking near me

NICE GREEN ENERGY

Home > News > Fracking near me

Search

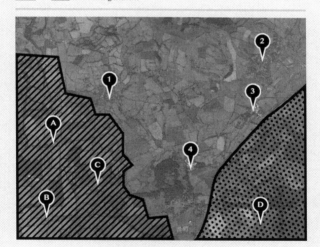

	Area	Date	Other fracking nearby
1	Abbey Fields	September 2016	MuckyGen www.muckygen.com
2	Brockenwocken	October 2017	
3	Chippersville	November 2018	OOOGEN www.ooogen.com
4	Devendslowe	December 2019	

Lastly, we have:

> <u>When</u> I want to find out what the government is saying about fracking
>> <u>I want to</u> see all the latest, relevant information easily and quickly
>>> <u>So I know</u> what the legal and political position is

You can see you have included:

- your audience's vocabulary (so they can find what they're looking for)
- your audience's mental models (so you can send them to other relevant, interesting content)
- techniques to help your audience read, understand, remember and act on your content

You are awesome and you're making the internet more useful and enjoyable.

NICE GREEN ENERGY

Government and fracking

Home > **News** > Government and fracking

We always comply with all of the government's shale oil and gas industry standards in our fracking operations.

Reports delivered to government

16 / 05 / 2014   **Nice Green Energy's submission to the Frackworthy report: UK-wide consultation on fracking**

30 / 07 / 2015   **Nice Green Energy's response to the white paper: fracking in clean cities**

18 / 09 / 2015   **Nice Green Energy's annual report**

For all government information on fracking please see the government's: shale oil gas and fracking information on the GOV.UK website.

N G E   Home   Our tariffs   News   Login

Caring for content

When you publish content, it is there forever. You might delete it, but that won't stop others screen-grabbing it and keeping it. That won't stop the Internet Archive (www.archive.org) taking digital copies. However, most organisations have a 'publish and forget about it' mindset – yours shouldn't.

You need to look after your content. Before you publish anything, you should know:
- what success is for that content
- when you are going to archive it
- when you are going to review it

So, for each piece of content you can agree, with stakeholders, the life cycle of this content.

Example:

Title: Government and fracking

Success: 10% increase every 6 months. (21.02.2017, minimum was 2,500 unique visits a month). If under this, we review.

Review: [content person's name] and [relevant expert's name] to review twice a year on [insert dates]

Archive: This content will be archived on [insert date] or after review assessment.

Success

You and your organisation needs to decide what success is. It could be traffic or number of sign-ups to your newsletter or use of links. It's different for all content for different organisations.

If you are setting these values for the first time, you can take a benchmark of what you have now (traffic, engagement, etc.) and either have that as a minimum or add a percentage to aim for.

Review

Always add names here. Make sure everyone in the process knows the content is their responsibility.

Archive

I always recommend having an archive (aka delete) date set when content is created. It focuses the mind of all involved in the creation process that you can't just publish and leave it.

Content has a lifespan. Don't let it fail and die and potentially embarrass you. Content needs to be cared for.

Content design

the end

is

not

the end

Content design isn't just a technique,

it's a way of thinking.

You'll question everything, gather data and make informed decisions.

You'll put your audience first.

So having done your research, designed your content and put it online – that's the end, isn't it?

Of course not. Go and start all over again with another piece of content.

And remember, if your content now isn't perfect because you had to compromise with a stakeholder, you are still further ahead than you were. One step at a time. Because of you, the internet is getting better.

This book was written to help you get started.

Your first steps may still feel daunting, and implementing content design in your organisation may still be difficult.

I've been there, I know what it's like.

Stick with it. Be persistent, be flexible, be bold.

Be confident that over time, content design will prove itself as a valuable tool for you, your team, and for the whole organisation.

Content design will help you achieve the most important goal: putting users first.

Get involved

Courses: contentdesign.london
Blog: contentdesign.london/blog
Twitter: @escmum

The content designer's checklist

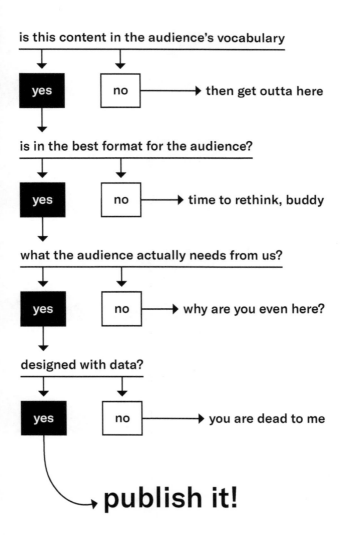

I am a content designer

And I am:
- awesome
- working for my audience
- loving my data (not in a weird way)
- creating an amazing experience for my audience

• silently correcting your grammar

The content designer's checklist

is this content in the audience's vocabulary

- **yes**
- no → then get outta here

is in the best format for the audience?

- **yes**
- no → time to rethink, buddy

what the audience actually needs from us?

- **yes**
- no → why are you even here?

designed with data?

- **yes**
- no → you are dead to me

→ publish it!

I am a content designer

And I am:
- awesome
- working for my audience
- loving my data (not in a weird way)
- creating an amazing experience for my audience

· silently correcting your grammar

Further reading, references, attributions

Forward

Content Strategy for the web
www.contentstrategy.com

The science of reading

pp32. Psychology of reading
https://books.google.co.uk/books?id=9eJ4AgAAQBA-
   J&printsec=frontcover

pp33. Erdmann and Dodge
https://en.wikipedia.org/wiki/Saccadic_masking

pp37. 'The effect of type size and case alternation on word identification' in the American Journal of Psychology
http://www.jstor.org/stable/1421250

pp37. 'Case alternation impairs word identification' in The Bulletin of
the Psychonomic Society
http://link.springer.com/article/10.3758/BF03333407

pp37. 'Not dumbing down' poster by Michael Thomas at Government
   Digital Service and Lorena Sutherland

Content discovery and research

pp64, pp65, pp66, pp67, pp68, pp69. Screenshots from
https://trends.google.com/trends/explore
&
www.google.co.uk

pp75. GOV.UK UK bank holiday page
https://www.gov.uk/bank-holidays

User stories and job stories

pp102. User stories vs job stories
https://jtbd.info/replacing-the-user-story-with-the-job-
story-af7cdee10c27

Designing content

pp132. BBC style guide
http://www.bbc.co.uk/academy/journalism/news-style-guide

pp132. GOV.UK style guide
https://www.gov.uk/guidance/style-guide

For more info on the story of content design in the British Government:
http://contentdesign.london/gov-uk/history-of-content-design-in-the-uk-government/

Thank you
Andrew Lamb, for introducing me to usability in the
first place. Without you, I would never have ended
up in GDS or written this book. Thank you for your
kindness and patience.

Kristina Halvorson
for the foreword,
encouragement and advice.

Sara Wachter-Boettcher
for the
amazing edit advice.

Chris McCarthy, for all the help with this book.
Michael Nottingham, for all his help with my blog
posts and this book.
Louise Stone for being an expert in user stories and
helping me with my training.
Julian Milne and Natalie Shaw for review help.
Emer Coleman for the mentoring and
unwavering support.
Chris Murphy, for keeping me going when I was going
to forget all about this book.
Tom Loosemore and Mike Bracken for my place in
GDS. Without you, content design would not be
a thing for me.
The original content design team at GDS. Thank you
for everything. Really. Everything.

And a very special thank you to:
Mum & Rich, for everything.
Giles, my amazing editor who turned this around.
You've made all this really work. Thank you.
Mark for the design - I LOVE IT.

To Ella, Stuart and Calum. I love you. You teach me something new every day. You are everything to me. Now, will you please put your shoes away?

For my dad. I miss you.

About the author

Sarah Richards grew up in Guildford, Surrey. She began her career as a researcher for a local TV company and then moved on to copywriting for Ogilvy & Mather and Saatchi & Saatchi.

After a few years doing commercial and local government websites, she ended up working for the Cabinet Office in the British government. In 2010, she created and led the GOV. UK content design team for the Government Digital Service (GDS).

Photo by Paul Clarke

In the process of moving 400 unwieldy and overcomplicated government websites into just one focused on user needs, Sarah and her fabulous team created the term 'content design' and the discipline outlined in this book.

Now, Sarah consults and runs training/coaching programmes with organisations and governments around the world.

You can contact Sarah on Twitter @escmum

ISBN: 978-1-5272-0918-3

Published in the United Kingdom by
          Content Design London
          Kemp House,
          152 City Road,
          London
          EC1V 2NX

Web   www.contentdesign.london
Email   info@contentdesign.london

First printed July 2017
Edited by Giles Turnbull
Design   Mark Hurrell
          This book is typeset using
          GT America & Suisse Works

Made in the USA
San Bernardino, CA
20 May 2019